GRAPHIC MODERN HISTORY: COLD WAR CONFLICTS

THE SOVIET WAR IN AFGHANISTAN

By Gary Jeffrey & Illustrated by Nick Spender

D1246099

Crabtree Publishing Company
www.crabtreebooks.com

Crabtree Publishing Company
www.crabtreebooks.com
1-800-387-7650

Publishing in Canada
616 Welland Ave.
St. Catharines, ON
L2M 5V6

Published in the United States
PMB 59051, 350 Fifth Ave.
59th Floor,
New York, NY

Published in **2014 by CRABTREE PUBLISHING COMPANY.**

All rights reserved. No part of this publication may be reproduced, stored in a retrieval system or be transmitted in any form or by any means, electronic, mechanical, photocopying, recording, or otherwise, without the prior written permission of copyright owner.

Printed in Hong Kong/092013/BK20130703

Copyright © **2013 David West Children's Books**

Created and produced by:
   David West Children's Books

Project development, design, and concept:
   David West Children's Books

Author and designer: Gary Jeffrey

Illustrator: Nick Spender

Editors: Lynn Peppas,
   Kathy Middleton

Proofreader: Kelly McNiven

Project coordinator:
   Kathy Middleton

Production coordinator and

Prepress technician:
   Ken Wright

Print coordinator:
   Margaret Amy Salter

Photographs:
   p4t, James A. Cudney, p4m,
   Cleric77; p5l, p7t, Erwin
   Franzen, p5b, p44b, Mikhail
   Evstafiev; p6t, DOD; p44m,
   Ronald Reagan Library, official
   government record; p45t, p45m,
   RIAN archive; p45b, RAWA;
   p47, Yuriy Somov

Library and Archives Canada Cataloguing in Publication

Jeffrey, Gary, author
   The Soviet war in Afghanistan / by Gary Jeffrey
and illustrated by Nick Spender.

(Graphic modern history : Cold War conflicts)
Includes index.
Issued in print and electronic formats.
ISBN 978-0-7787-1235-0 (bound).--ISBN 978-0-7787-1239-8
(pbk.).--ISBN 978-1-4271-9346-9 (pdf).--ISBN 978-1-4271-
9342-1 (html)

   1. Afghanistan--History--Soviet occupation, 1979-
1989--Juvenile literature. 2. Afghanistan--History--Soviet
occupation, 1979-1989--Comic books, strips, etc. 3.
Graphic novels. I. Spender, Nik, illustrator II. Title.
III. Series: Jeffrey, Gary. Graphic modern history. Cold
War conflicts

DS371.2.J45 2013   j958.104'5   C2013-904133-8
                                C2013-904134-6

Library of Congress Cataloging-in-Publication Data

Jeffrey, Gary.
  The Soviet War in Afghanistan / by Gary Jeffrey and
Illustrated by Nick Spender.
    pages cm. -- (Graphic modern history: Cold War
conflicts)
  Includes index.
  ISBN 978-0-7787-1235-0 (reinforced library binding) -- ISBN
978-0-7787-1239-8 (pbk.) -- ISBN 978-1-4271-9346-9 (electronic
pdf) -- ISBN 978-1-4271-9342-1 (electronic html)
  1. Afghanistan--History--Soviet occupation, 1979-1989--
Comic books, strips, etc. 2. Afghanistan--History--Soviet
occupation, 1979-1989--Juvenile literature. 3. Graphic novels.
I. Spender, Nik, illustrator. II. Title.

DS371.2.J43 2014
958.104'5--dc23

                   2013023910

CONTENTS

STATE OF CHAOS

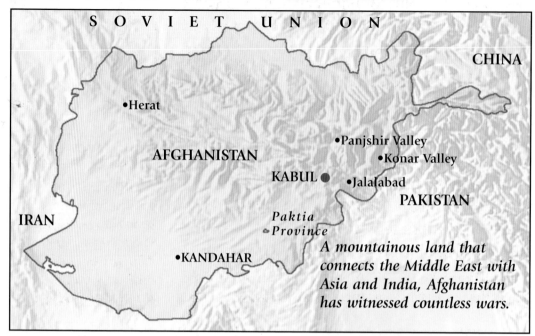

SOVIET UNION

CHINA

•Herat

AFGHANISTAN

•Panjshir Valley
•Konar Valley

KABUL ● •Jalalabad

PAKISTAN

IRAN

Paktia
Province

•KANDAHAR

A mountainous land that connects the Middle East with Asia and India, Afghanistan has witnessed countless wars.

In 1979, the Soviet Union invaded its unstable neighbor Afghanistan and installed a communist government. To remove Soviet influence from that region, the United States and other countries gave support to the Afghan rebels, escalating Cold War tensions.

Daud seized power from his cousin, King Zahir, to become Afghanistan's first-ever president.

FROM MONARCHY TO REPUBLIC

Mohammad Daud Khan, former prime minister of Afghanistan, took power in a bloodless coup in 1973. He changed Afghanistan into a socialist republic. By 1977, Daud's communist opponents had grown stronger under Soviet influence. Daud then sought closer ties with Saudi Arabia, Iran, and even the West but was assassinated.

Daud died in a hail of bullets, on April 28, 1978, when the Afghan army was directed to storm the palace. The assassination was kept secret from the public. The new president, Nur Mohammad Taraki (left), was a fanatical communist.

REPRESSION

New president, Nur Mohammad Taraki, based the new Democratic Republic of Afghanistan (DRA) on the Soviet Union's earlier communist model under the iron-fisted leader Josef Stalin. In Afghanistan, the Islamic religion was suppressed, land was forcibly redistributed, but equality for women was granted. The mainly tribal, fiercely traditional, country people protested. Resistance by guerilla "fighters for the faith," called Mujahideen, broke out in 25 of 28 provinces.

Meanwhile, Prime Minister Hafizullah Amin overthrew Taraki and made himself president. Amin tried to stop the Mujahideen by softening his policies, but the damage was done.

Amin had been the leader of the communist People's Democratic Party of Afghanistan (PDPA). He had Taraki arrested and killed.

Widespread defection from noncommunists in the army continued to strengthen the Afghan jihad, or holy war.

"THE BEAR" STEPS IN

Amin had lost control of the countryside and even parts of the capital, Kabul. Afghanistan seemed destined to become an Islamic state. Across the border the Soviets readied for action. Around-the-clock flights took paratroopers into Kabul airport, and on December 27, 1979, two motorized Soviet divisions invaded Afghanistan.

After a battle at the Darulaman Palace, Amin surrendered and was executed by paratroops. He had been in power for just three months.

BRUTE FORCE

The Soviets flew in Babrak Karmal, an exiled leader of the Afghan communist party, to be president. He became a puppet ruler of Afghanistan—the newest satellite Soviet state.

Soviet paratroops patrol Kabul in 1979, alert for any possible uprising.

GOING IT ALONE

Soviet armed forces occupied the main cities, communications, and air bases. The rebellion had spread, and there was mass desertion from the Afghan army to the Mujahideen. Although the United States opposed the spread of communism, the Soviets were confident that America would not become involved. It would be too unpopular at home.

The Soviets believed the combined power of their helicopter gunships and ground armor would smash the rebels' will to fight.

SWEEPING CLEAN

Motorized units supported by helicopter-borne troops were sent in to sweep valleys clear of the Mujahideen. Reluctant to dismount from their armored vehicles, Soviet soldiers put their faith in their massive fire power. This allowed the rebels, who knew the terrain, to hide and ambush Soviet troops at will, causing heavy casualties. The Mujahideen would then retreat to safe territory.

The invasion united different cultural groups against a common enemy. What they lacked in organization and equipment (in the early years), they made up for in fighting skills honed through years of internal blood feuding against one another.

BLOODIED BUT UNBEATEN

Wherever the Soviets thought the Mujahideen were hiding, bombers and helicopters would strike, destroying villages and crops to drive away the civilian population. This "depopulation" was intended to deny the Mujahideen supplies and safe places to hide. But these armed civilians had no permanent bases and were constantly moving. Only in the northern Panjshir Valley was there any kind of full-time, regular army.

Guerrillas in this valley were a direct threat to the capital, Kabul. Between 1980 and 1985, the Soviets launched nine offensives to try to clear it. But guerrilla leader Ahmad Shah Massoud remained undefeated, earning him the legendary nickname, the "Lion of Panjshir."

Below, Mujahideen return to a village totally destroyed by Soviet air strikes.

FIREFIGHT IN THE BATTLE FOR KAMA

THE VILLAGE OF SAMA CARAY, NEAR KAMA, EASTERN AFGHANISTAN, FEBRUARY 15, 1983. MUJAHIDEEN COMMANDER ABDUL BAQI BALOTS WOKE TO THE SOUND OF HELICOPTERS.

THUCKA!
THUCKA!
THUCKA!

THERE ARE SO MANY OF THEM. THIS DOESN'T LOOK GOOD!

CALM YOURSELF, HAJI. IF WE DIE TODAY, SO BE IT.

FROM HIS VILLAGE, BALOTS WATCHED A GROUP OF FIGHTERS MAKE A RUN FOR THE MOUNTAINS.

SOVIET PARATROOPS POSITIONED ON THE HIGH GROUND TO THE NORTH DREW A BEAD...

...AND CUT DOWN TWO OF THEM.

BANG!
BANG!
BANG!

BANG!
BANG!

AARRRRRGH!

GNNNGH!

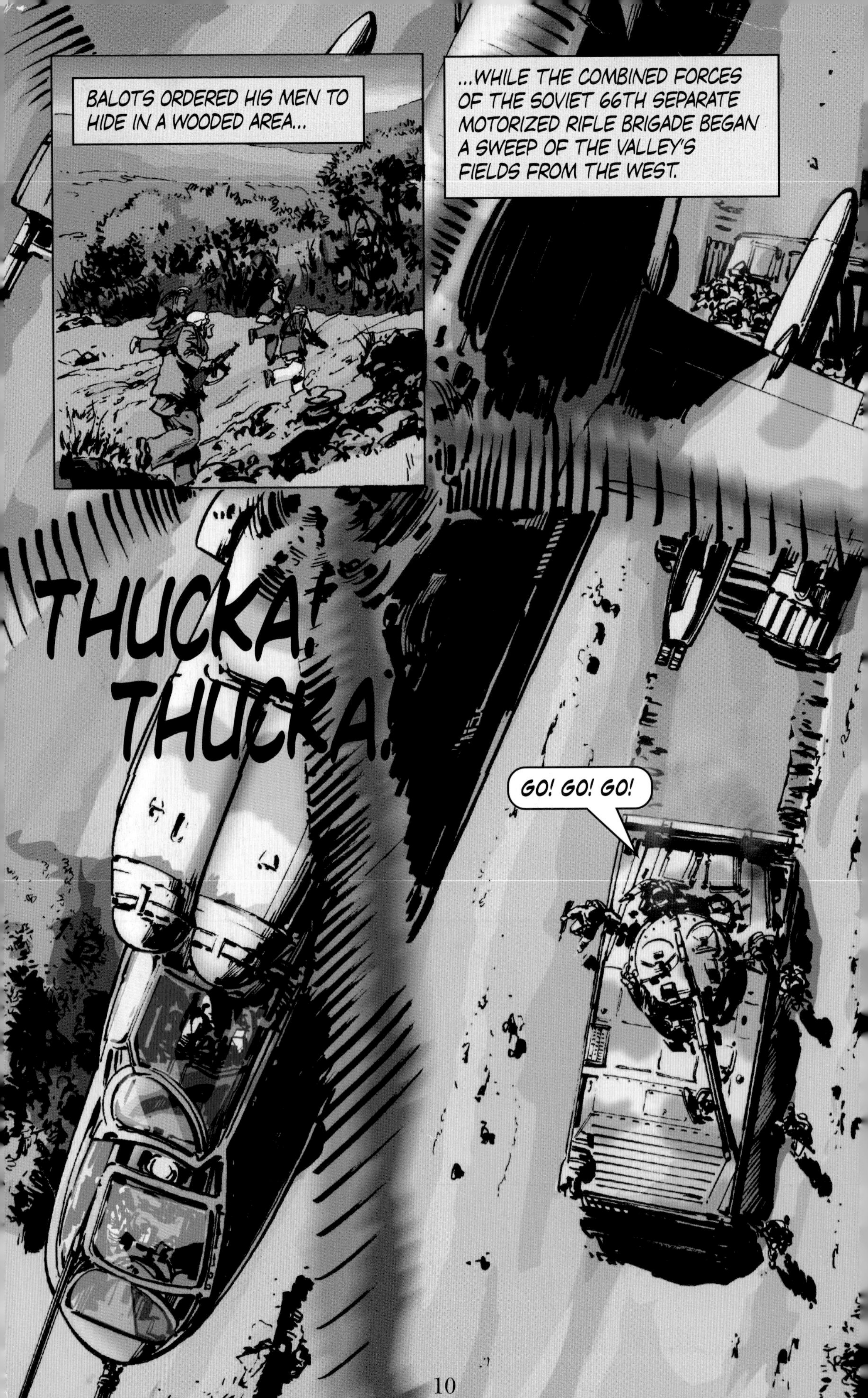
BALOTS ORDERED HIS MEN TO HIDE IN A WOODED AREA...
...WHILE THE COMBINED FORCES OF THE SOVIET 66TH SEPARATE MOTORIZED RIFLE BRIGADE BEGAN A SWEEP OF THE VALLEY'S FIELDS FROM THE WEST.
THUCKA! THUCKA!
GO! GO! GO!

BY 1500 HOURS, THE SOVIET FORCES WERE APPROACHING.

FORWARD!

A CIVILIAN CAME TO SEE BALOTS.

YOU'VE GOT TO GET OUT OF HERE BEFORE THEY SET THE WOODS ON FIRE!

NO! I CAN'T LEAVE THESE PEOPLE...

...THEY'LL BE BURNED ALIVE!

MOST OF THE VILLAGERS WERE ALSO CONCEALED IN THE TREES.

THE LEAD SOVIET ARMOR TANK SUDDENLY VEERED NORTH TOWARD KAMA.

BRRRUUM! BRRRUUM!

WITH NO RADIOS, BALOTS'S MEN HAD TO SEND MESSENGERS.

SOVIET ASSAULT TROOPS ARE MOVING TOWARD MASHINGAN!

THEY WILL NEED TO CROSS THE BRIDGE!

BALOTS ARRANGED HIS MEN ON EITHER SIDE OF THE BRIDGE.

SUDDENLY, THEY WERE SPOTTED.

PEEOW!

KRAK!

MY RIFLE! WHAT WILL I DO NOW?

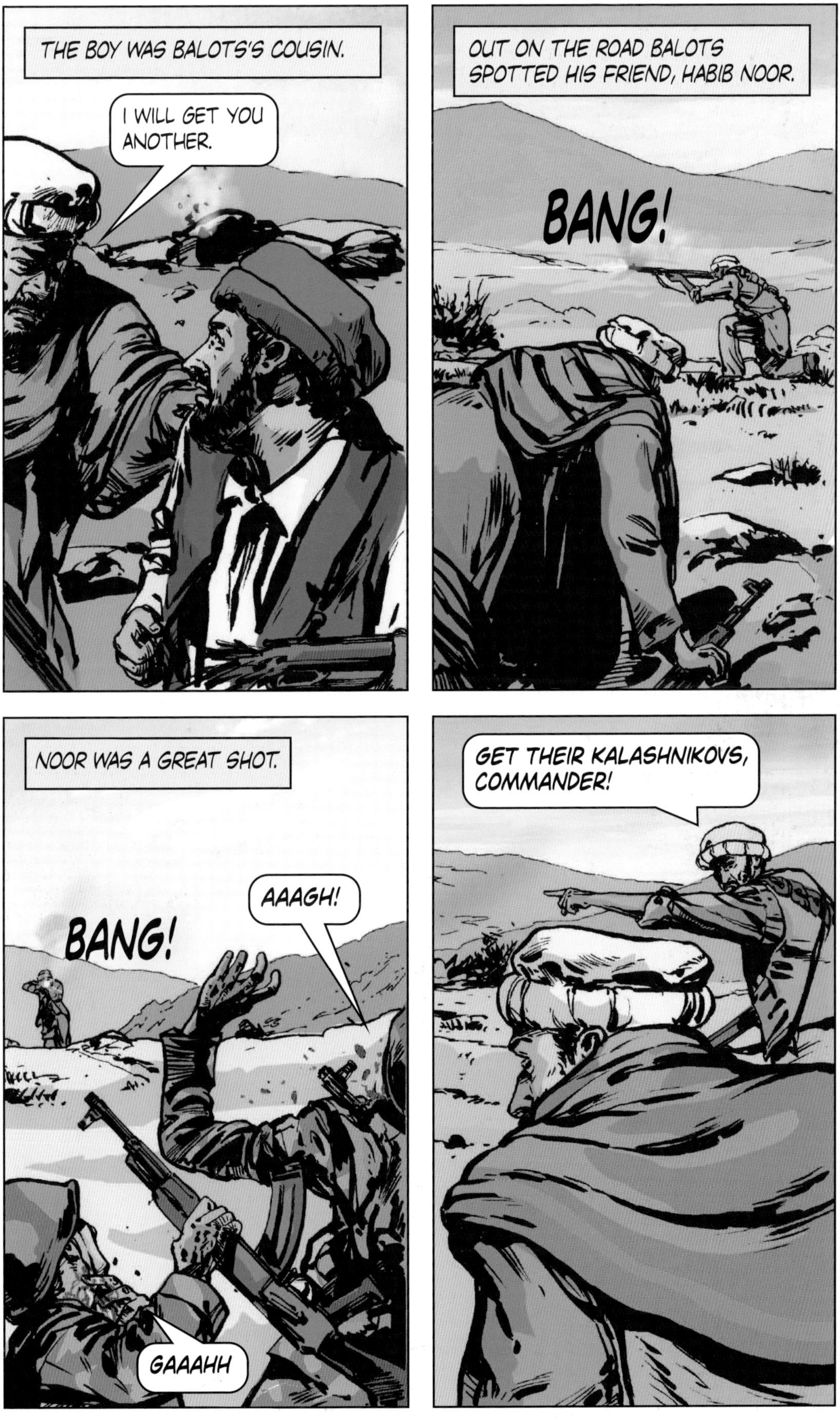
THE BOY WAS BALOTS'S COUSIN.
I WILL GET YOU ANOTHER.
OUT ON THE ROAD BALOTS SPOTTED HIS FRIEND, HABIB NOOR.
BANG!
NOOR WAS A GREAT SHOT.
BANG!
AAAGH!
GAAAHH
GET THEIR KALASHNIKOVS, COMMANDER!

BALOTS SPRINTED TO THE BODIES AND TRIED TO PULL AN ASSAULT RIFLE FREE.

GNNNNGH! NO GOOD – IT'S STUCK FAST!

ENEMY BULLETS TORE THROUGH THE SPACES IN HIS BAGGY TROUSERS.

HE WAS PINNED. IN DESPERATION BALOTS PULLED THE PIN AND TOSSED AN RKG* ROUND.

NEED A DIVERSION.

THE LOUD NOISE OF THE ANTI-TANK GRENADE DISTRACTED HIS ATTACKERS.

BANG!

HE REJOINED NOOR.

WE'VE GOT TO CROSS THE STREAM OR WE WON'T BE ABLE TO **GET AT THEM**.

YOU'RE SHORTER THAN ME SO THEY WON'T SEE YOU.

HABIB, I AM YOUR COMMANDER, BUT I AM UNDER **YOUR** COMMAND NOW!

*AN ANTI-TANK GRENADE

15

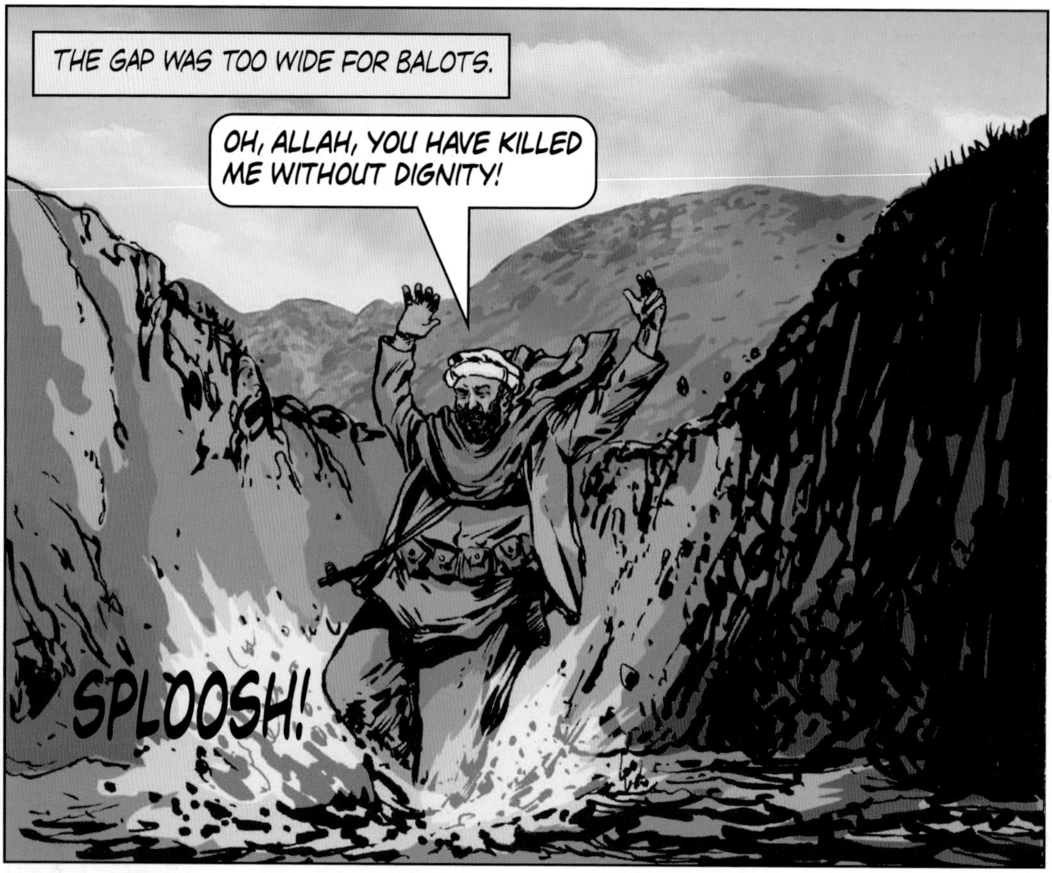
THE GAP WAS TOO WIDE FOR BALOTS.
OH, ALLAH, YOU HAVE KILLED ME WITHOUT DIGNITY!
SPLOOSH!

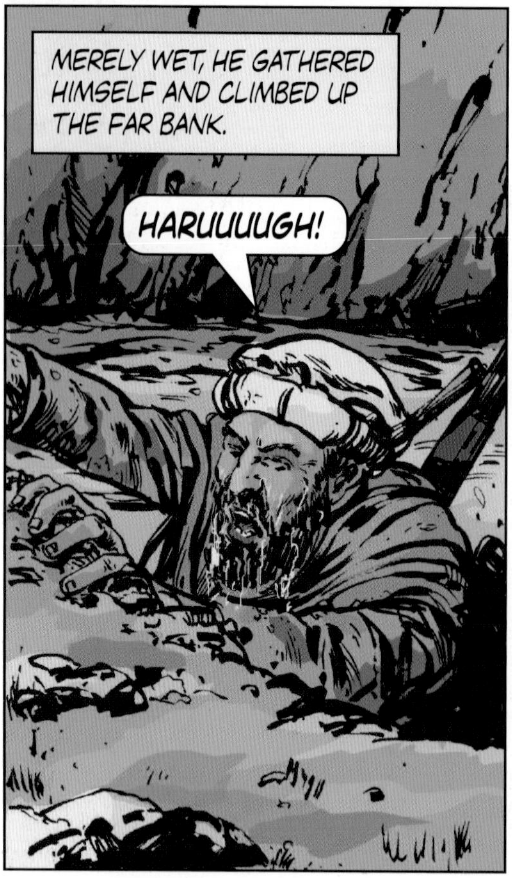
MERELY WET, HE GATHERED HIMSELF AND CLIMBED UP THE FAR BANK.
HARUUUUGH!

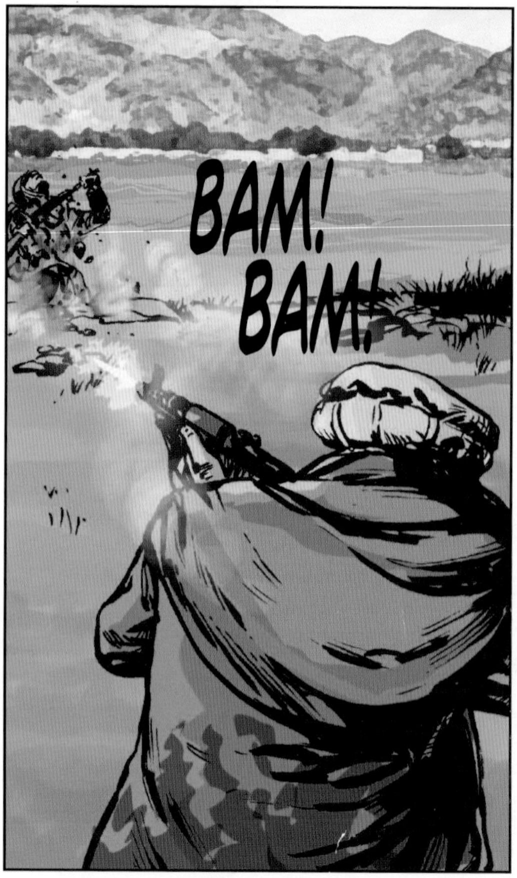
BAM! BAM!

NOOR HAD MADE IT ACROSS TOO.

OVER THERE! THEY'RE IN THE HOUSES!

BALOTS LET OUT A RIP OF BULLETS WITH HIS AK-47...

BANG-BANG-BANG-

...AND THREW GRENADES.

BOMPH!

HE LOOKED AROUND AT NOOR.

SURRENDER, YOU DOGS!

GET DOWN OR YOU'LL GET YOURSELF—

A BULLET PIERCED NOOR'S GUT.

UNNNGH...

BALOTS'S FRIEND DIED IN HIS ARMS.

NO!

SIR, TAKE THIS!

THE RPG* FELL AMONG THE INFANTRY, HALTING THEIR ADVANCE.

BOOM

PHWOOOSH!

*ROCKET-PROPELLED GRENADE

IT WAS A CHANCE TO BREAK OFF CONTACT. WRAPPING NOOR'S BODY IN A TSADAR*, THEY HURRIED AWAY FROM THE BATTLEFIELD.

LATER, BALOTS HIRED A CAMEL TO TAKE NOOR'S BODY BACK TO HIS HOME.

HE WAS NOT EVEN FROM OUR VILLAGE. HE WAS FROM THE AHMADZAI.

THE END

*ALL-PURPOSE CLOTH WORN AS EVERYDAY CLOTHING.

ASSAULT ON THE PANJSHIR VALLEY

APRIL 30, 1984, THE SOVIET 682ND MOTORIZED RIFLES HAD BEEN ORDERED TO CLEAR A RAVINE THAT LED OFF FROM THE PANJSHIR VALLEY.

ISN'T THE COMMANDER GOING TO SEND SOME TROOPS UP TO TAKE THE HEIGHTS FIRST?

NO, THERE'S NO NEED.

LOOK AT IT. QUIET AS A TOMB, JUST LIKE THE MAIN VALLEY. NO ONE HOME.

THE MUJAHIDEEN HIDDEN ON THE ROCK TERRACE AIMED THEIR RIFLES AND BEGAN TO FIRE...

BLAM-BLAM

KRACK!

THE SOUND OF THE AMBUSH ECHOED BACK DOWN TO THE REGIMENTAL COMMAND POST.

CRACK! CRACK! RUMBLE

THE BATTALION HAS BEEN ATTACKED. WE MUST GET THE WOUNDED AND DEAD.

PRIVATE NIKOLAI KNYAZEV HELPED LOAD STRETCHERS ONTO THEIR ARMORED VEHICLES.

SOUNDED LIKE ONE HECK OF A FIREFIGHT.

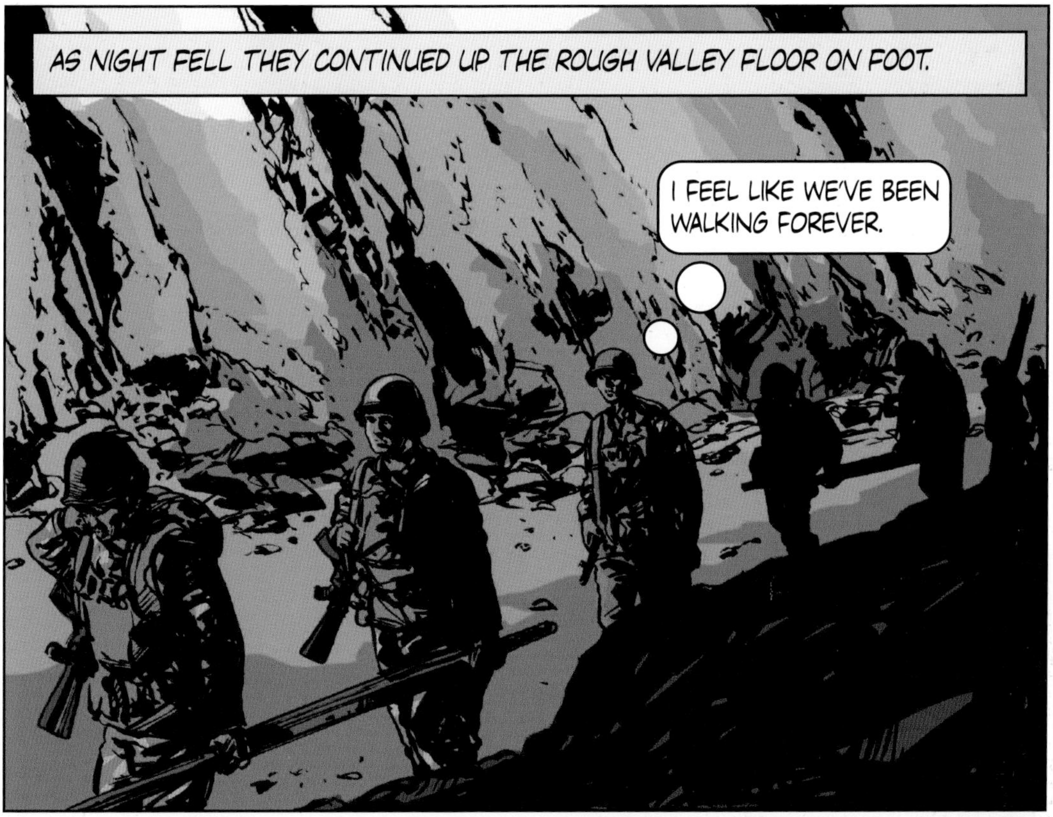
AS NIGHT FELL THEY CONTINUED UP THE ROUGH VALLEY FLOOR ON FOOT.
I FEEL LIKE WE'VE BEEN WALKING FOREVER.

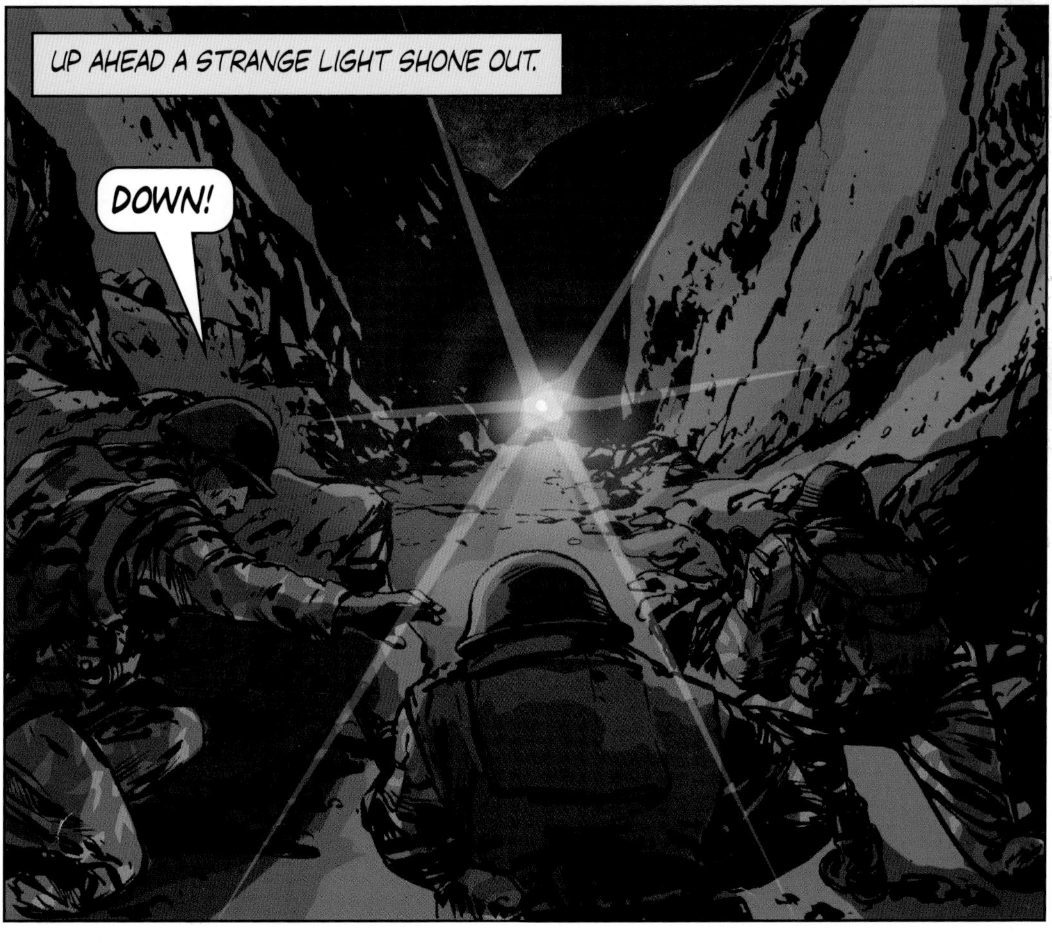
UP AHEAD A STRANGE LIGHT SHONE OUT.
DOWN!

A KALASHNIKOV RANG OUT.

BANG!
BANG!

BULLETS FLEW OVER THEIR HEADS.

THE LIGHT'S FROM A TURRET PERISCOPE!

HEY! HEY! STOP FIRING! WE'RE FRIENDLY!

KNYAZEV'S PLATOON COMMANDER SENT UP A FLARE.

FWOOOSH

THE FIRING CEASED.

THE VEHICLE, A BMP, HAD BEEN DISABLED. TWO OF THE BATTALION HAD STAYED WITH IT.

...HIT BY A MINE! GET THEM OUT OF THERE!

FARTHER ON, THEY MET AN ELITE SQUAD WHO HAD GONE ON AHEAD, RETURNING WITH...

WHO IS IT?

KOROLEV.

...BODIES...

THE *CAPTAIN*?!

DAWN BEGAN TO BREAK AS THEY WENT DOWN THE MAIN STREET OF A KISHLAH.*

BRRRMM

MOTORS?

26

*A RURAL SETTLEMENT

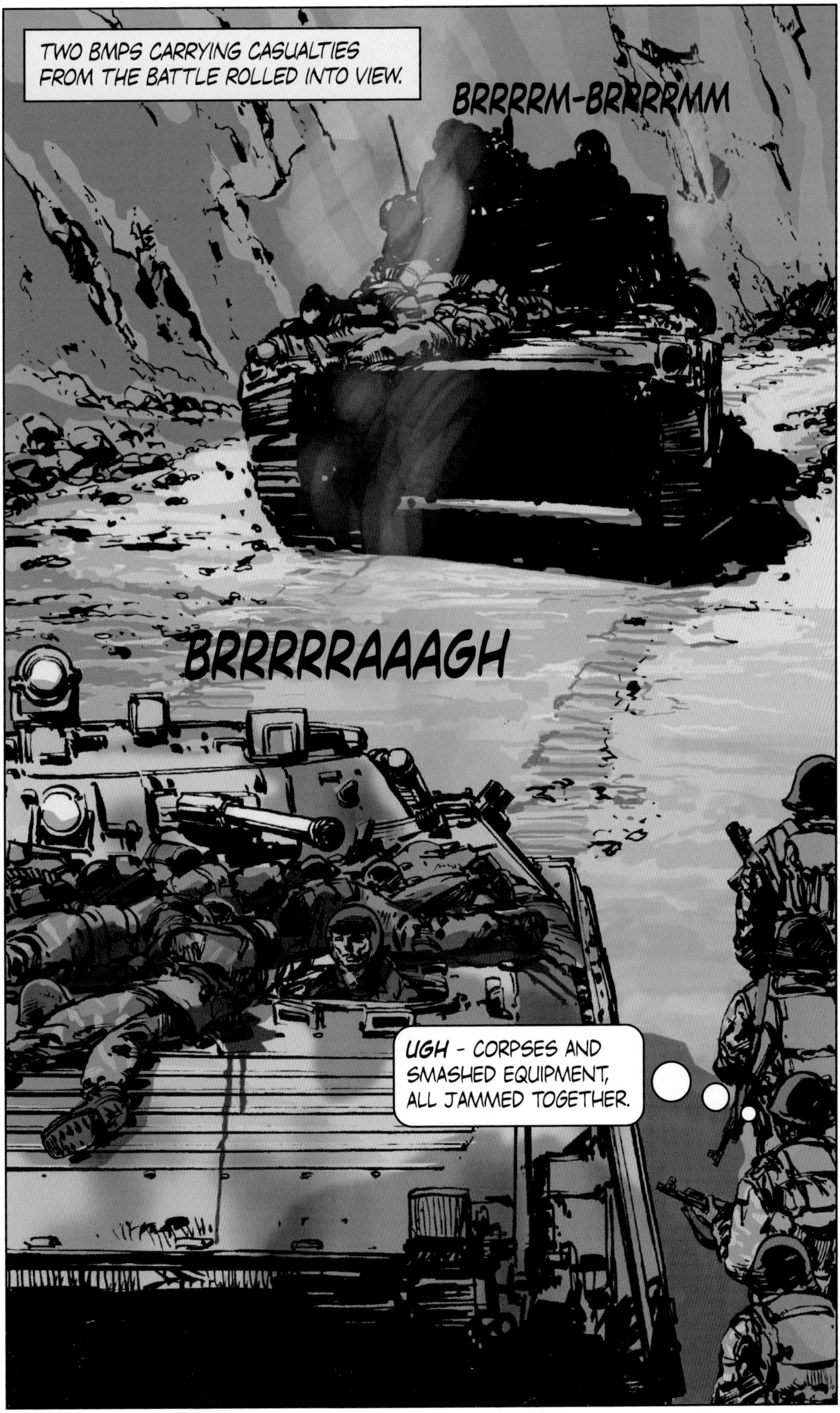
TWO BMPS CARRYING CASUALTIES FROM THE BATTLE ROLLED INTO VIEW.
BRRRRM-BRRRRMM
BRRRRRAAAGH
UGH - CORPSES AND SMASHED EQUIPMENT, ALL JAMMED TOGETHER.

BEHIND THEM CAME SURVIVORS.

BOZHE MOI.* LOOK AT THE FACES OF THOSE MEN.

WHAT HAVE THEY BEEN THROUGH?

*OH, MY GOD.

THE SURVIVORS WERE TAKEN BACK TO THE COMMAND POST. SOON A GENERAL ARRIVED.

WHUP WHUP WHUP

FORM UP! FORM UP!

PULL YOURSELVES TOGETHER!

HOW CAN THEY? THEY STILL STINK OF DEATH.

A VISITING OFFICER BERATED THE MEN.

YOU USELESS MEN ARE JUST STANDING HERE WHILE YOUR COMRADES ARE LYING OUT THERE! WHY ARE YOU HERE?

KNYAZEV WAS PART OF A SQUAD SENT BACK UP THE RAVINE TO RETRIEVE THE REST OF THE BATTALION.

OH, THE STINK! THIS IS THE PLACE ALRIGHT.

KNYAZEV FOUND A GROUP OF SIX YOUNG SOLDIERS PILED UP IN FRONT OF A CAVE ENTRANCE.

EITHER MACHINE-GUNNED OR GRENADED AS THEY SOUGHT REFUGE.

BZZZZZZZZ

BZZZZZZZZ

OTHERS HAD BEEN BLOWN AWAY COMPLETELY.

NOTHING LEFT BUT SHREDS OF UNIFORM.

THEN FROM BEHIND SOME ROCKS...

URRRRRRR...

IT WAS THE LAST SURVIVOR.

HEY!

DESPITE LOSING HIS SHIN, THE SOLDIER HAD MADE A TORNIQUET AND STOPPED THE BLEEDING.

HOLD STILL!

WATER!

IT WAS TIME TO CLEAR OUT.

GENTLY! GENTLY! GO EASY!

EVERY SINGLE WEAPON HAS BEEN TAKEN BY THE REBELS.

MAY 2. THEY RETURNED TO THE MAIN VALLEY WHERE THE DEAD WERE LAID OUT PRIOR TO EVACUATION.

HERE LIES LIEUTENANT KURDIUK, OUR COMPANY COMMANDER.

SAID TO HAVE BEEN MURDERED BY REGULAR AFGHAN SOLDIERS WHEN THEY DESERTED TO THE MUJAHIDEEN.

THE END

STINGER vs HIND

FOR SEVEN LONG YEARS HEAVILY ARMORED SOVIET MI-24 HIND HELICOPTER GUNSHIPS HAD BEEN ABLE TO KILL AND MAIM AFGHAN FIGHTERS AND CIVILIANS AT WILL FROM THE SKIES.

WHUP-WHUP-WHUP

PEEEOW

PEEEOW

BANG

BANG

IT'S NO GOOD. OUR BULLETS ARE JUST BOUNCING OFF!

RUN!

THE SOVIET PILOTS CALLED THEMSELVES "GRAY WOLVES."

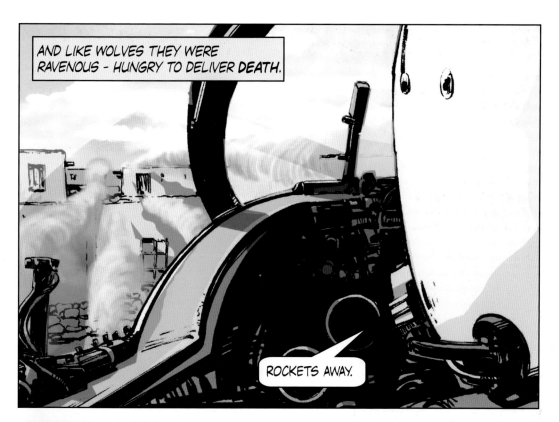

AND LIKE WOLVES THEY WERE RAVENOUS - HUNGRY TO DELIVER **DEATH**.

ROCKETS AWAY.

THE MUJAHIDEEN HAD NO WAY TO DIRECTLY TAKE ON THE FEARSOME WEAPON THEY CALLED "GARBOK"*...

DRRRRRRRRRR

...UNTIL NOW...

*BOOGIE MAN

SEPTEMBER 26, 1986, NEAR JALALABAD, MUJAHIDEEN FIGHTER ABDUL WAHAB KNELT IN PRAYER. NEXT TO HIM LAY THE LAUNCHER OF AN FIM-92A STINGER MISSILE, SUPPLIED COVERTLY BY THE AMERICAN CIA.

GOD, LET ME BE FRUITFUL.

WAHAB AND TWO OTHERS, ZALMAI AND GHAFFAR, HAD BEEN SENT TO PAKISTAN AND TRAINED TO USE THE SURFACE-TO-AIR MISSILES.

SOME DISTANCE AWAY FROM THEIR FIELD A LARGE FLIGHT OF MI-24S WAS RETURNING TO THE SOVIET AIRBASE FROM A SORTIE.

TODAY WOULD BE THEIR FIRST TEST IN COMBAT.

WAHAB SHOULD GO FIRST. HE WAS THE BEST IN TRAINING.

DO IT RIGHT, ABDUL. A LOT IS RIDING ON THIS!

IF THEY WERE SUCCESSFUL, THE AMERICANS WOULD SUPPLY MORE MISSILES. IF NOT...

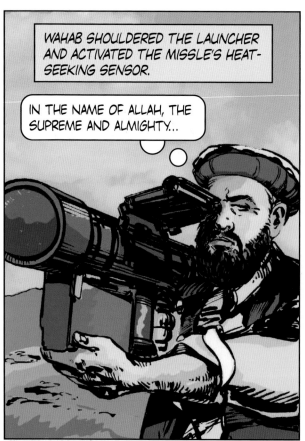

WAHAB SHOULDERED THE LAUNCHER AND ACTIVATED THE MISSLE'S HEAT-SEEKING SENSOR.

IN THE NAME OF ALLAH, THE SUPREME AND ALMIGHTY...

HE HAD 40 SECONDS OF BATTERY POWER TO FIND AND LOCK ONTO A TARGET.

...GOD IS GREAT.

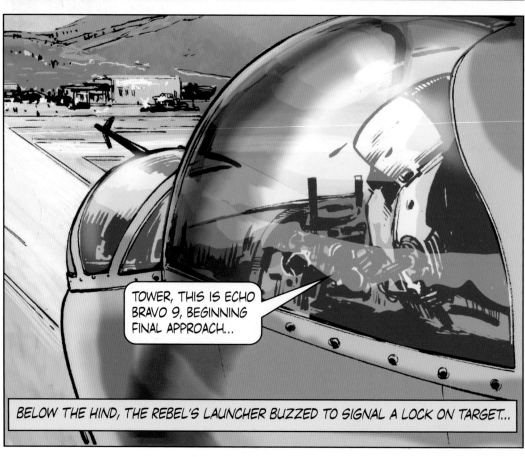

TOWER, THIS IS ECHO BRAVO 9, BEGINNING FINAL APPROACH...

BELOW THE HIND, THE REBEL'S LAUNCHER BUZZED TO SIGNAL A LOCK ON TARGET...

...AND WAHAB PULLED THE TRIGGER.

FOOOOSH!

AFTER CLEARING THE LAUNCHER, THE MISSILE EXTENDED ITS FINS AND BLASTED AWAY AT TWICE THE SPEED OF SOUND...

SWOOOSH!

...HOMING IN ON THE LEAD HIND'S EXHAUST.

AS IT NEARED THE AIRCRAFT, A PROXIMITY FUSE* DETONATED, EXPLODING THE WARHEAD AND COMPLETELY SHEARING OFF THE MI-24'S TAIL.

KROOM

THE TAILLESS CRAFT BURST INTO FLAMES...

*A PROXIMITY FUSE EXPLODES A DEVICE WHEN IT REACHES A CERTAIN DISTANCE

...AND SLAMMED INTO THE RUNWAY.

AS THE MUJAHIDEEN CHEERED, ZALMAI ALSO FIRED, SENDING HIS MISSILE USELESSLY INTO THE GROUND.

PLOMP

ALLAHU AKBAR!* ALLAHU AKBAR!

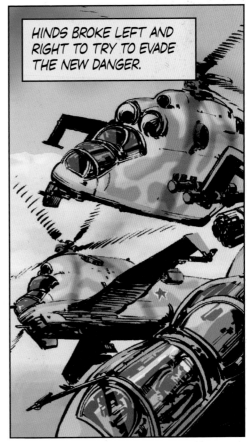

HINDS BROKE LEFT AND RIGHT TO TRY TO EVADE THE NEW DANGER.

*GOD IS GREAT.

41

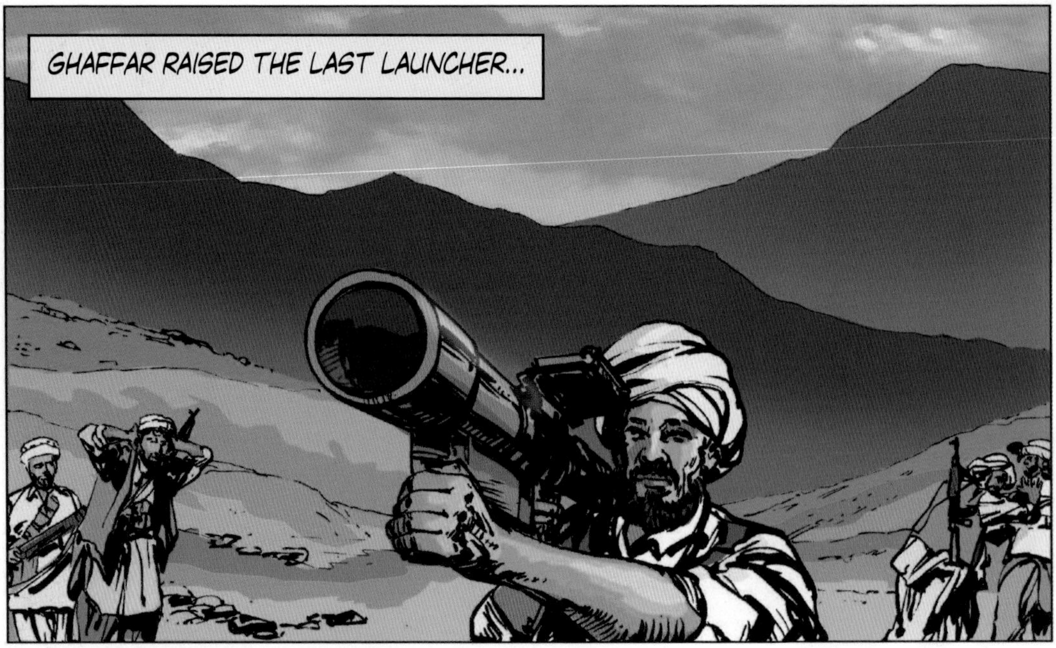
GHAFFAR RAISED THE LAST LAUNCHER...

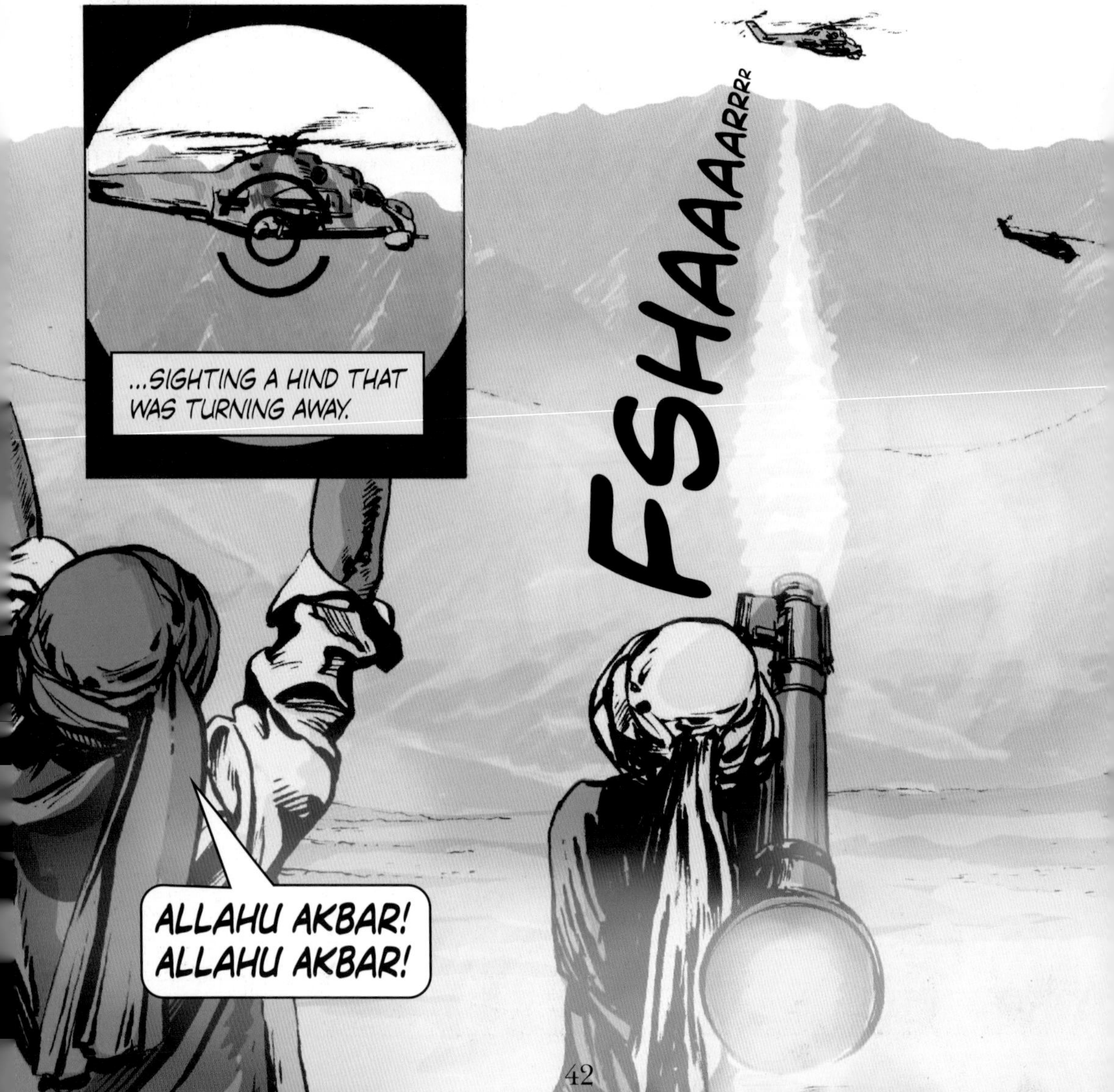
...SIGHTING A HIND THAT WAS TURNING AWAY.
FSHAAAARRRR
ALLAHU AKBAR! ALLAHU AKBAR!

THE PANIC-STRICKEN SOVIET PILOTS NEVER KNEW WHAT HIT THEM...

SHSSSSSSSS

...AS THE STINGER RUPTURED THEIR FUEL TANK, CREATING A MASSIVE FIREBALL.

THE END

EXIT WOUNDS

U.S. congressman Charlie Wilson, seen here meeting Mujahideen, helped arrange for Stinger missiles to be supplied to the resistance via Pakistan.

U.S. President Ronald Reagan found the cause of the Afghans "...an inspiration to those who love freedom," and a chance to roll back Soviet influence.

"There are only two things the Afghans must have: the Koran and Stingers."—Ahmad Shah Massoud, 1987

RUSSIA'S VIETNAM?

Over the course of the war, the United States spent up to twenty billion dollars supplying rebels with nine hundred Stinger missiles and 250 launchers, along with other arms.

A withdrawal of Soviet forces had been planned since the rise of Soviet leader Mikhail Gorbachev in 1985. Gorbachev wanted to improve the Russian economy and the Afghan conflict was a great drain. The war was unpopular with ordinary Russians, and worldwide media coverage was also harming international Soviet relations.

In 1986, the Soviets began transferring the burden of fighting the rebels onto Afghan (DRA) forces. The first Soviet troops went home in 1987.

COLD WAR THAW

Over seven years, more than 14,400 Soviet soldiers had been killed in battle and 53,000 wounded. Afghan army losses were 18,000 dead. Up to 90,000 Mujahideen had died along with up to 1.5 million Afghan civilians. Armed with the best weapons and training, the Soviets were beaten by rebels who were prepared to fight indefinitely.

In 1989, the last Soviet forces left Afghanistan. Two years later, the Soviet Empire broke up, ending the Cold War.

Soviet President Mikhail Gorbachev oversaw Glasnost—the opening up of Soviet Russia.

Soviet veterans arriving home often wondered what the fighting had been for.

Bloody civil war broke out in 1992, as militant Islamists bombarded Kabul with rockets to try to bring down the new moderate Islamic government.

AFTERMATH

The war had left five million refugees, most set up in camps in Pakistan. Religious schools in these camps would spawn the future Taliban—Afghanistan's extreme Islamic political group.

The battle continued between the rebels and the Soviet-supported Kabul regime until it fell in 1992. In the civil war that followed, moderates led by Massoud eventually defeated the militants. In 1996, with the country in ruins, the Taliban defeated the militants.

GLOSSARY

Allah Arabic for the one true God of Islam

ambush A sudden attack combined with the element of surprise

blood feuding Bitter and continuous feuding between members of families or clans

BMP A Soviet amphibious, tracked, infantry fighting vehicle

casualties Civilians or soldiers in hostile engagements that die, are captured, or go missing

CIA Central Intelligence Agency—one of the principal intelligence-gathering agencies of the United States federal government

civilian A citizen who is not fighting in the army

Cold War A period of political tension from 1947 to 1990 during which communist countries led by the Soviet Union and democratic countries from the West led by the United States competed militarily. Each side tried to control or influence unstable countries around the world in an effort to spread their own styles of government.

communist Someone who believes a political philosophy that says everyone should be treated equally and share all goods equally

coup An overthrow of a government, usually by a group determined to replace it with another body, either civil or military

covertly Not done or made openly

defection To leave one country, army, or organization for another

desertion Tthe abandonment of a "duty"or post without permission

draw a bead Take aim

elite squad Highly-trained special forces

firefight A brief exchange of fire

friendly A military term describing forces fighting on the same side

grenade A small bomb that can be thrown by hand

guerrillas Forces not part of the regular army

ideologies Sets of beliefs that form the basis of political or economic systems

infantry Forces who fight on foot

Islam The religion or faith based on God's messages to Muhammad

Islamic state A form of government in which all laws are based on the religion of Islam

Kalashnikov (AK-47) A type of assault rifle developed in the U.S.S.R.

Koran Islam's holy book

militants People whose political beliefs are extreme

moderates People whose political beliefs are not extreme

monarchy A form of government in which the leader inherits power

Mujahideen Rebel fighters from different ethnic groups in Afghanistan who fought against Soviet-led Afghan forces in Afghanistan

offensives Carefully planned military attacks

puppet ruler A ruler under a foreign government control

repression The control by force of citizens' actions and free speech

resistance A movement fighting against control by foreign powers

satellite state An independent country that is economically or politically influenced or controlled by another country's government

socialist republic A government in which citizens have the right to vote, but most property and resources are controlled by the state

sortie A short flight into enemy territory on a military mission

Soviet Empire An informal term that encompassed the regions of the Soviet Union (including Russia) and its satellite states

Stinger A portable, infrared, homing, surface-to-air missile

suppressed Prohibited by law or force

surface-to-air Weapons launched from the ground at targets in the air

Taliban A political movement of Islamic militants in Afghanistan

tourniquet A tightly wrapped bandage used to stop bleeding

tribal Loyal to a common social group, usually made up of families

turret periscope A device on a tank's gun mount that provides a view of an object that is above or below direct sight

warhead The part of a missile that contains the explosive

international troops prepare to leave Afghanistan, in 1986.

47

INDEX